# AMERICAN PROVERBS

ֶ

# AMERICAN PROVERBS

ֶ

Compiled by Judith Reitman

Illustrated by Barbara Smolover

HIPPOCRENE BOOKS, INC.
*New York*

ISBN 0-7818-0753-0

For information, address:
HIPPOCRENE BOOKS, INC.
171 Madison Avenue
New York, NY 10016


Printed in the United States of America

# INTRODUCTION

In any language, a proverb can be defined as "a well-known truth expressed as a maxim." It is a succinct, memorable statement that contains advice, *Don't marry for money, but don't marry without money*; a warning or prediction, *Beware of him who has nothing to lose*; or an observation, *Man's best friend is his dog*.

American proverbs are unique in their reflection of particular regional attitudes and affectations. Take, for instance, a warning in Arkansas to meet life head-on: *It takes gizzards and guts to get along in the world*. A similar sentiment in New Mexico may be: *If you don't C sharp, you'll B flat*. And, in Vermont: *The world is your cow, but you have to do the milking*.

As in every language, proverbs often contradict themselves: *Great ambitions make great men*, and the contrary *Ambition destroys its possessor*. For those contemplating matrimony: *It isn't a life without a wife*, while for some, *A ring on your finger is one in your nose*.

Here, then, are some choice truths from the United States. Choose among them whatever suits your mood or time in life. Enjoy!

# CONTENTS

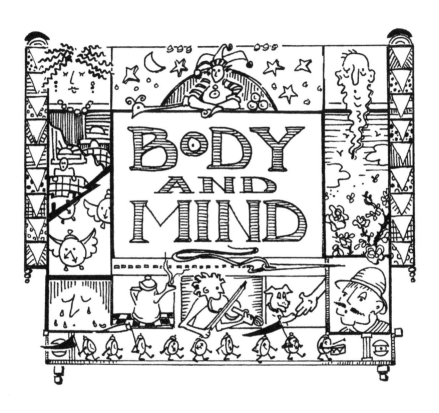

Advice To A Fool Goes In One Ear And Out The Other

# ᛋᛃ Advice ᛃᛋ

We hate those who will not take our advice and
despise those who do.

Advice is cheap.

Advice is least heeded when most needed.

Advice is not a popular thing to give.

Ask advice, but use your own common sense.

Good advice is beyond price.

He asks advice in vain who will not follow it.

We should never be too proud to take advice.

Many receive advice but only the wise profit from it.

Never advise a man to the halter or altar.

It's easier to be critical than correct.

Don't kick a man when he's down.

# ❧ Age ❧

A woman is as old as she admits.

You can't teach an old dog new tricks.

Old age is an incurable disease.

One is as old as one's heart.

You can be as old as Methuselah and still be a fool.

Age before beauty.

Older and wiser.

Age breeds aches.

Age is no excuse for foolishness.

Age and marriage tame man and beast.

Age mellows some people; others it makes rotten.

With age comes wisdom.

A man is as old as he feels, a woman as old as she looks.

There's no fool like an old fool.

You're only young once.

The older the fiddle, the better the tune.

❧

# ❧ Beauty ❧

Beauty is only skin deep.

Beauty without virtue is a rose without fragrance.

A thing of beauty is a joy forever.

She who is born beautiful is born married.

Beauty and folly are old companions.

Beauty and brains don't mix.

Beauty is as beauty does.

Beauty doesn't make the pot boil.

Beauty is one of God's gifts.

Beauty is the flower of life, but virtue is the fruit.

Beauty's tears are only skin deep.

Beauty comes from within.

There's no beauty like the beauty of the soul.

Beauty draws more than oxen.

Beauty's only skin deep, but ugly goes to the bone.

A fair face may hide a foul heart.

❧

# ❧ Health ☙

Good health is above wealth.

If you lack health, you lack everything.

Health is better than wealth.

An apple a day keeps the doctor away.

The best physicians are Dr. Diet, Dr. Quiet, and Dr. Merryman.

He who would live long avoids excesses.

The doctor is often more to be feared than the disease.

Good health is priceless.

Early to bed, early to rise, makes a man healthy, wealthy and wise.

He who goes to bed thirsty, rises healthy.

Afflictions are sometimes blessings in disguise.

❧

# ❧ Knowledge ❧

We don't know when we are well off.

All that we know is that we know nothing.

He knows enough who knows how to mind his own business.

The man who knows most, forgives most.

A little knowledge is a dangerous thing.

Zeal without knowledge is the sister of folly.

Lose all, but find yourself.

To be proud of knowledge is to be blind and light.

Knowledge wanes but wisdom lingers.

❧

# ❧ Mind ❧

A busy mind breeds no evil.

A contented mind is a continual feast.

A sound mind, a sound body.

A willing mind makes a light foot.

Put the impossible out of your mind.

A ruffled mind makes a restless pillow.

Great minds run in the same channel and
weak ones in the same gutter.

Out of sight, out of mind.

Every woman has the right to change her mind.

A mind made up is no mind at all.

A good mind possesses a kingdom.

Two minds are better than one.

Mind is the great lever of all things.

The mind of the man is the man.

Everyone complains of his memory but no one complains
of his judgement.

❧

*An idle mind is the devil's workshop.*

# ❧ Time ❧

In this world, nothing is permanent except change.

All things change and we with them.

The more it changes, the more it remains the same.

All good things come to an end.

There is a time to speak and a time to remain silent.

The third time is a charm.

Time flies.

Time heals all wounds.

Time is money.

The first one hundred years are the hardest.

One of the greatest labor-saving inventions of today is tomorrow.

Time will pass.

Time never stands still.

Time marches on.

Time will tell.

Never do today what you can put off until tomorrow.

Never put off until tomorrow what you can do today.

Have a good time; but if you can't be good, be careful.

These are the times that try men's souls.

Keep ahead of the times. Lost time is never found again.

Tomorrow never comes.

Years know more than books.

A stitch in time saves nine.

Everything has its time.

Time and tide wait for no man.

Anytime means no time.

Time is the best healer.

Time is a hard taskmaster.

Sleep on it.

Time works wonders.

Never waste time.

There must be a first time for everything.

Life is short and time is swift.

There's no time like the present.

Time brings everything to those who wait.

# ৯ Wisdom ৶

It needs great wisdom to play the fool.

A word to the wise is sufficient.

You can't put old heads on young shoulders.

Wisdom never lies.

Nine-tenths of wisdom consists in being wise in time.

The doors of wisdom are never shut.

A wise man has wise children.

With age comes wisdom.

It takes gizzards and guts to get along in the world.

It's a wise man who holds his peace.

An ounce of wisdom is worth a pound of wit.

If you don't C sharp, you'll B flat.

Still tongue, wise head.

Horse sense is just stable thinking.

Great minds run in the same channels.

Wise men make proverbs and fools repeat them.

The head can save the heels.

Still waters run deep.

Wisdom is better than rifles.

Wise men learn by other men's mistakes; fools by their own.

Wealth may seek us, but wisdom must be sought.

Early to bed, early to rise, makes a man healthy, wealthy and wise.

৯

# ✌ Childhood ✌

A bitten child dreads a dog.

Daughters are brittle ware.

A good son is the light of the family.

Who has no son has no satisfaction.

A child must learn to crawl before it can walk.

Spare the rod and spoil the child.

Every mother's child is handsome.

Every girl is beautiful in her father's eyes.

The least boy always carries the greatest fiddle.

Like father, like son.

Deacons' daughters and ministers' sons are the biggest devils
that ever run.

You can tell a lot about the size of a boy by what he loses his head over.

A child needs love the most when he deserves it the least.

A quiet child is plotting mischief or has done it.

It's a wise child that knows its own father.

Boys will be boys.

Girls will be girls.

As the boy is, so is the man.

If boys were meant to smoke they'd have chimneys on their heads.

You can take a boy out of the country, but you can't take the
country out of the boy.

Teach a child to hold its tongue; he will learn fast enough to speak.

The child is father of the man.

*Little boys are made of
rats and snails
and puppy dog tails.*

*Little girls are made of
sugar and spice
and everything that's nice.*

Boys seldom make passes for girls who wear glasses.

Every time a boy goes wrong, a good man dies.

The great man is he who does not lose his child's heart.

There are four things every child needs: an abundance of love, plenty of good nourishing food, lots of soap and water, and after that some good healthy neglect.

Little boys who play with matches get their fingers burned.

The future of a child is the work of the mother.

Once a bad boy, always a bad boy.

What a child does at home, it will do abroad.

When a child is little, it pulls at your apron strings. When it gets older, it pulls at your heartstrings.

You can always tell a youngest child, but you can't tell him much.

Children are poor man's riches.

Children are to be seen and not heard.

Children, chickens and women never have enough.

Don't slap your children in the face,
for the Lord prepared a better place.

It takes children to make a happy home.

The devil could not be everywhere, so he made children.

Little children, little troubles; big children, big troubles.

# ✥ Family ✥

First a daughter, then a son, and the family's well begun.

A family is a twosome that grows some.

The family who prays together, stays together.

Mistakes happen in the best families.

The family of fools is very old.

Some families are like potatoes; all that is good of them is underground.

*There's a black sheep
in every family.*

# ❧ Father ☙

Father knows best.

The father is the head, but the mother is the heart.

A miserly father makes a prodigal son.

Honor your father and your mother.

As the baker, so the buns; as the father, so the sons.

The father to his desk, the mother to her dishes.

When a father praises his son, he flatters himself.

A boy's friend is his father.

# ✀ Friendship ✀

Friendship cannot live with Ceremony, nor without Civility.

A friend in need is a friend indeed.

A false friend is worse than an open enemy.

There are three faithful friends: an old wife, an old dog, and ready money.

Friends tie their purses with spider's thread.

A faithful friend is better than gold.

A friend in the market is better than money in the purse.

Make new friends but keep the old.

Fire is the test of gold, adversity of friendship.

When friends meet, hearts warm.

Beware of fair weather friends.

A friend is easier lost than found.

Short reckoning make long friends.

A good friend is my nearest relation.

A friend married is a friend lost.

A friend to all is a friend to none.

Friendship is love with understanding.

Be slow in choosing a friend, slow in changing.

A friend whom you can buy can be bought from you.

A man is known by his friends.

A man's best friend is his ten fingers.

Before you make a friend, eat a peck of salt with him.

Choose your friends like your books, few but choice.

Cultivate friends who pray for you, not prey upon you.

Fall sick and you will know who is your friend and who is not.

Friends slowly won are long held.

Man's best friend is his dog.

If you want a friend, you will have to be one.

Old friends are best.

One does not make friends, one recognizes them.

Never drop the friends you made on the way up. You may need them
on the way down.

Never trust a friend who deserts you in a pinch.

Speak well of your friends, of your enemies say nothing.

God sends us our relatives but we can choose our friends.

Being friendly doesn't cost anything.

A blazing friendship goes out in a flash.

Your best friend is yourself.

Friendship is a two-way street.

Sudden friendship, sure repentance.

A common enemy makes friends.

Fortune makes friends, misfortune tries them.

He who laughs at others' woes finds few friends and many foes.

# ❧ Home ❧

Home is the father's kingdom, the children's paradise,
the mother's world.

Men build houses, women build homes.

Home sweet home.

Home is where the heart is.

A man's home is his castle.

There's no place like home.

It takes two to make a home.

Not all houses are homes.

You can build a house, but you have to make a home.

No roof can cover two families.

Four walls do not make a home.

# ❧ Mother ❧

Sweet talk the mother to get the daughter.

A mother wants her daughter married well, but her sister doesn't
want her married better than she is.

Mother knows best.

As is the mother, so is the daughter.

Mother's love is best of all.

The hand that rocks the cradle rules the world.

No mother has a homely child.

A girl's friend is her mother.

God could not be everywhere, so He made mothers.

If you take a child by the hand, you take a mother by the heart.

There is only one good mother-in-law, and she is dead.

# ✌ Love ✌

Love is blind.

Love lasts as long as money endures.

Love makes the world go round.

Love laughs at locksmiths.

Love will find a way.

As is the lover, so is the beloved.

You can't live on love alone.

Love, a cough, smoke, and money can't long be hid.

The course of true love never did run smooth.

Once a lover, always a lover.

Love is a little sighing and a little lying.

Love at first sight is cured by second look.

First love, last love, best love.

Blind love mistakes a harelip for a dimple.

He who forces love where none is found remains a fool
the whole year round.

Love 'em and leave 'em.

You haven't lived if you haven't loved.

Love your neighbor as yourself.

All's fair in love and war.

All mankind loves a lover.

True love never grows old.

Puppy love leads to a dog's life.

You always hurt the one you love.

Opposites attract.

One never appreciates what he has until he had lost it.

Lovers are fools.

# ❧ Marriage ❧

Don't marry without love, but don't love without reason.

Don't marry for money, but don't marry without money.

He who marries for money earns it.

Marry first and love will follow.

Marry your son when you will and your daughter when you can.

Many a good hanging prevents a bad marriage.

Borrowed wives, like borrowed books, are seldom returned.

A man who kicks his dog will beat his wife.

Marriages are made in heaven.

Early wed, early dead.

A good son makes a good husband.

Keep your eyes wide open before marriage; afterwards, half shut.

Maids want nothing but husbands, and when they have them,
they want everything.

A ring on your finger is one in your nose.

There's no help for misfortune but to marry again.

When a man marries, his life begins.

A son's a son until he takes a wife, but a daughter's a daughter
all her life.

Marry late or never.

Gentlemen prefer blondes but marry brunettes.

Men are always wooing goddesses and marrying mere mortals.

A man is newly married who tells his wife everything.

A man chases a woman until she catches him.

To marry once is a mistake; to marry twice, fatal.

A man doesn't want a woman smarter than he is.

A man is king in his own home.

It's better to be an old man's sweetheart than a young man's slave.

Men are born the slaves of women.

A good wife and health are a man's best wealth.

It isn't a life without a wife.

# ɔa Men ʚɔ

You can't keep a good man down.

You can't live with men, neither can you live without them.

Men walk backwards like crabs and think they are making progress.

No man is so old but thinks he may live another day.

No man is an island.

A man can be led but he can't be driven.

A man can die but once.

All men are created equal.

A man is no better than his word.

A man is as strong as his will.

The bigger the man, the bigger the mark.

Man cannot live by bread alone.

It's the easiest thing in the world for a man to deceive himself.

A man can do no more than he can.

It's a wise man who knows his own mind.

A man is known by the company he keeps.

As a man thinks, so he is.

Don't be a 'yes' man.

Every man dies as he must.

Every man has a fool up his sleeve.

Every man has a price.

*A* man should not
stick his nose in his neighbor's pot.

Every man must sow his wild oats.

Every man must stand on his own two feet.

Every man to his own poison.

Every man to his taste.

A man can't be hanged for his thoughts.

Man is the only animal that can be skinned more than once.

A man cannot live to himself alone.

Men who talk by the yard and think by the inch should be removed by the foot.

A man is as young as he feels.

Don't send a boy on a man's errand.

Men are best loved further off.

# ✣ Sex ✣

Lust never sleeps.

As polite as a whore at a christening.

Nervous as a whore in church.

Nervous as a pregnant prostitute in church.

Stands out like a whore in church.

When the cat's away, the mice will play.

When the husband's away, the wife will play.

Kissing a man without a mustache is like eating egg without salt.

Jealousy will get you nowhere.

We can resist everything except temptation.

The strongest oaths are straw to the fire in the blood.

No man has learned the art of life till he has been well-tempted.

If a man is unfaithful to his wife, it's like spitting from a house into the street. But if a woman is unfaithful to her husband, it's like spitting from the street into the house.

✣

# ✺ Women ✺

The last generation will be female.

A woman's tongue is only three inches long,
but it can kill a man six feet high.

A good girl always gets caught; a bad girl knows how to avoid it.

Praise a maid in the morning and the weather in the evening.

Man works from sun up to sun down,
but a woman's work is never done.

Woman rules man but the devil rules her.

A woman never forgets her first love.

There is no mischief but a woman is at the heart of it.

Women and dogs set men together by their ears.

Man gets and forgets; woman gives and forgives.

Maidens should be mild and meek, swift to hear and slow to speak.

The only secret a woman can keep is that of her age.

Women and elephants never forget.

Women are the devil's nets.

Man is the head, but woman turns it.

Trust your dog to the end, and a woman to the first opportunity.

You can never tell about a woman, but if you can, you shouldn't.

Women will have the last word.

A skinny woman's like a racehorse: fast and fun
but no good for work.

*Man reigns, but a woman rules.*

A woman is a dish for the gods.

A woman is only a woman; a good cigar is a smoke.

A woman's hair is her crowning glory.

Women would be more charming if one could fall into their arms
without falling into their hands.

A lady is a woman who makes it easy for a man to be a gentleman.

Behind every great man there is a great woman.

A little bit of powder and a little bit of paint
make a woman look like she ain't.

❧

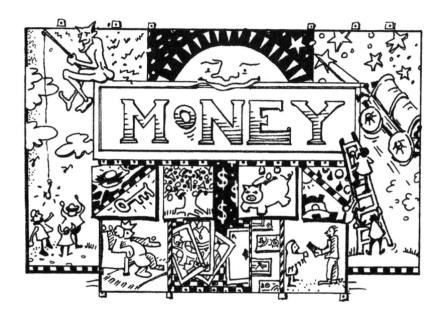

# ❧ Ambition ❧

A man without ambition is like a woman without looks.

Ambition and fleas jump high.

Ambition is the last infirmity of noble minds.

Hitch your wagon to a star.

Ambition loses many a man.

The higher they climb, the steeper they fall.

Nothing seek, nothing find.

Ambition destroys its possessor.

Ambition is putting a ladder against the sky.

Great ambitions make great men.

Success has many parents, but failure is an orphan.

Man's ambition knows no bars; with vision he carves his way
to the stars.

Opportunities, like eggs, come one at a time.

If you don't have a plan for yourself, you'll be a part of
someone else's.

Ambition is no cure for love.

People who get to the top are not afraid of uphill work.

❧

# ❧ Avarice ❧

Ambition often spends foolishly what avarice has collected wickedly.

Avarice generally miscalculates and as generally deceives.

Avarice is the root of all evil.

Many a man thinks he is buying pleasure when he is really selling
himself a slave to it.

Avarice loses all in seeking to gain all.

The road to ruin is kept in good repair, and
the travelers pay the expense.

Gambling is the son of avarice and the father of despair.

There's no vice like avarice.

# ❧ Credit and Debt ❧

Nothing travels faster than a bad check.

A man who gives credit loses friends, money and customers.

Credit is suspicion asleep.

Credit makes enemies.

Credit breeds discredit.

He who drinks on credit gets double drunk.

Rather go to bed supperless than run in debt for breakfast.

No man's credit is as good as his money.

The other face of credit is debt.

Your credit is worth more than your capital.

Early to rise and late to bed lifts again the debtor's head.

Seldom loan comes laughing home.

Creditors have better memories than debtors.

Money borrowed is soon sorrowed.

Pay your debts or lose your friends.

A man in debt is caught in a net.

He robs Peter to pay Paul.

Without debt, without care.

Out of debt, out of danger.

Debt is the worse poverty.

Debt is a hard taskmaster.

*You can run into debt, but you have to crawl out.*

A small debt makes a debtor; a heavy one, an enemy.

The man in debt is a jump ahead of the sheriff.

# ❧ Dollar ❧

A bad dollar always comes back.

A dollar in the bank is worth two in the band.

A dollar saved is a dollar made.

Don't waste ten dollars looking for a dime.

If you keep a dollar in your pocket you'll never go broke.

Lend a dollar, lose a friend.

You can't get dollars by pinching nickels.

Your best friend is your dollar.

Another day, another dollar.

I had rather be a beggar and spend my last dollar like a king
than be a king and spend my money like a beggar.

Pennies make dollars.

Don't hold the dimes so near your eye that you can't see the dollar.

A quick nickel is better than a slow dollar.

Save a dollar and keep your worries away.

# ❧ Generosity ❧

Our generosity should never exceed our abilities.

Generosity is more charitable than wealth.

The generous are always just and the just are always generous.

Better to give than to lend.

Measure a man by what he gives as well as by what he does.

Give a little, take a little.

Give and you shall receive.

He gives doubly who gives happily.

He who gives twice is blessed.

It is better to give than to receive.

It is not only what we give, but how we give it that counts.

Let him who gives nothing be silent, and him who receives speak.

Not what we give, but what we share makes us great.

# ✌ Gold ✌

A man may buy gold too dear.

All that glitters is not gold.

A golden key opens every door, except that of Heaven.

An inch of gold cannot buy an inch of time.

Even if it rained gold, a lover would never become rich.

Gold dust blinds all eyes.

Gold is tested by fire, men by gold.

Gold is the devil's fishhook.

Gold is the snare of the soul.

Gold is where you find it.

Gold rules the world.

Gold will not buy everything.

He that can catch and hold, he is the man of gold.

Gold, women and linen should be chosen by daylight.

It is gold that greases the wheel of love.

When gold speaks, other tongues are dumb.

When we have gold, we are in fear; when we have more,
we are in danger.

Where there is gold, there the devil dwells.

An ass covered with gold is more respected than
an ass covered with a packsaddle.

No ear is deaf to the song that gold sings.

# ❧ Greed and Envy ❧

Greed breeds contempt.

Big mouthfuls often choke.

Greed killed the wolf.

Greed overreaches itself.

Greed to need does surely lead.

Give the hog a finger and he'll take the whole hand.

Feed a pig and you'll have a hog.

The grass is always greener on the other side.

Don't wish too hard; you might just get what you wish for.

❧

Greedy folks have long arms.

# ❧ Money ❦

Don't spend all your money in one place.

Don't throw good money after bad.

Bad money always comes back.

In God we trust. All others pay cash.

Many people will sell their souls for money.

Any fool may make money, but it takes a wise man to keep it.

He that is of the opinion money will do everything
may well do everything for money.

Money is power.

Money greases the axle.

Money talks, everything else walks.

It's better to tell your money where to go than ask where it went.

Never spend your money before you have it.

Money can't buy happiness, but it sure makes misery easier
to live with.

Put your money where your mouth is.

Nothing but money is sweeter than honey.

Don't take any wooden nickels.

The rich get richer, the poor get babies.

People are funny about money.

Money begets money.

Much coin, much care.

Money burns a hole in the pocket.

Put not your trust in money, but put your money in trust.

Save your money and die rich.

Money doesn't grow on trees.

Money doesn't make the man.

The best way to double your money is to fold it and
put it in your pocket.

Money in the purse will always be in fashion.

Money is honey, my little sonny, and a rich man's joke is
always funny.

Ready money is ready medicine.

Money is like manure: it's only good when spread around.

Money is the universal language speaking any tongue.

When a man says money can do anything,
it's a sure sign he hasn't got any.

Better spent than spared.

Money is the root of all evil.

Money isn't everything in life.

Money makes the world go round.

Money recommends a man everywhere.

Money saved is money earned.

Who puts up the money does the talking.

A fool and his money are soon parted.

❧

# ✺ Penny ✺

A bad penny always comes back.

A hard-earned penny is a well-earned penny.

A penny in the hand is worth two in the pot.

A penny saved is a penny earned.

A penny today is worth two tomorrow.

A single penny fairly got is worth a thousand that are not.

An honest penny is worth a stolen dollar.

In for a penny, in for a pound.

One penny is better than none.

Penny-wise, pound-foolish.

Save your pennies for a rainy day.

Take care of your pennies and the dollars will
take care of themselves.

Who will not keep a penny shall never have many.

You can tell a bad penny by its ring.

✺

# ❧ Poverty ❧

Of all poverty, that of the mind is the most deplorable.

Poverty gives a man strange bedfellows.

Poverty has no kin.

Poverty is no crime.

Poverty is no sin.

When I eat with the children of poverty my heart sleeps.

Poverty is not a shame, but being ashamed of it is.

Poverty is the mother of crime; want of sense is the father.

Poverty makes a hog gentle.

Poverty makes good fellowship.

Poverty and love are hard to hide.

God helps the poor, the rich help themselves.

He is poor but he is proud.

Poverty of mind is often concealed under the garb of splendor.

Poverty, poetry and new title of honor make men ridiculous.

Poverty is the mother of all the arts.

Poor men's tables are soon spread.

The poorest man in the world is he who has nothing but money.

Poverty is the mother of invention.

The poor must dance as the rich pipe.

Poverty shows us who our friends are and who are our enemies.

There is no virtue that poverty does not destroy.

When poverty comes in the door, love goes out the window.

Old age and poverty are wounds that can't be healed.

Sloth is the mother of poverty.

What is the matter with the poor is poverty.

# ❧ Thrift and Spending ❧

Most people consider thrift a fine virtue in ancestors.

Thrift is to a man what chastity is to a woman.

Practice thrift or else you'll drift.

He who spends more than he should shall not have to spend
when he would.

Spend and God will send.

Who spends before he thinks will beg before he dies.

# ❧ Wealth ❧

Halving your wants quadruples your wealth.

A man of wealth is a slave to his possessions.

Command your wealth, else it will command you.

He who loses wealth loses much;
he who loses even one friend loses more;
but he that loses his courage loses all.

It is not wealth but wisdom that makes a man rich.

Sudden wealth is dangerous.

A first wealth is health.

Wealth and content are not always bedfellows.

Wealth is best known by want.

Wealth is like rheumatism: it falls on the weakest parts.

Wealth, like want, ruins many.

Wealth makes many friends.

Wealth and power do not give peace of mind.

Where genius, wealth and strength fail, perseverance will succeed.

The thoughts of the heart, these are the wealth of a man.

Virtue is everlasting wealth.

Early to bed, early to rise, makes a man healthy, wealthy and wise.

❧

# ᔆ Work ᔆ

A work ill done must be done twice.

All work and no play makes Jack a dull boy.

He who has a trade has an estate.

All work is noble.

Chase your work or your work will chase you.

Do work well or not at all.

Do your own work and know yourself.

Hard work conquers the worst of luck.

Hard work is the best investment a man can make.

If you want work well done, select a busy man.

It's all in a day's work.

Nothing worth having ever comes without a lot of hard work.

The best way to get rid of work is to do it.

The only work that hurts a man is hopeless work.

The works of man will perish.

The world is your cow, but you have to do the milking.

Work beats worry.

Work before play.

Work is the only capital that never misses dividends.

Little wit in the head makes much work for the feet.

Work is work if you're paid to do it, and it's a pleasure if you pay to be allowed to do it.

Work never hurt any man.

Worry kills more men than work.

Work keeps you out of mischief.

Many hands make light work.

Unless you work hard, you cannot succeed.

It must be hard to work, but it must be harder to want.

The best way to kill time is to work it to death.

Better to beg than to steal, but better to work than to beg.

Man works from sun to sun, but a woman's work is never done.

Whistle while you work.

# ❧ Birth and Death ❧

Birth is much, but breeding is more.

No man can help his birth.

Death and life are in the power of the tongue.

A man of high birth may be of low worth, and vice versa.

Better death than dishonor.

There is remedy for everything except death.

Death cannot kill what never dies.

Death fiddles and we dance.

Speak well of the dead.

Never say die!

Six feet of earth makes all men equal.

The dead are soon forgotten.

You can't take it with you.

We're here today and gone tomorrow.

When we're dead, we're dead for a long time.

Death is a great leveler.

Every door may be shut but death's door.

Nothing is certain except death and taxes.

Men fear death as children do going in the dark.

Dead men tell no tales.

Death waits for no one.

The death of one dog is the life of another.

Old men go to death, but death comes to young men.

When death knocks at your door, you must answer.

# Evil

See no evil, hear no evil, speak no evil.

Avoid evil and it will avoid you.

Choose the lesser of the two evils.

Destroy the seed of evil or it will grow in your truth.

Desperate evils require desperate measures.

Evil is brought on by one's self.

He who does evil comes to an evil.

One evil breeds another.

One rotten apple spoils the barrel.

He who does evil suspects evil on the part of his fellow man.

Of the two evils, choose the prettiest.

We cannot do evil to others without doing it to ourselves.

Nothing is evil, but thinking makes it so.

Evil gotten, evil spent.

Crime does not pay.

# ❧ Faith and Hope ❧

Where there's a will there's a way.

If you don't keep faith with man, you can't keep faith with God.

A good hope is better than a bad possession.

Hope keeps the heart from breaking.

Every cloud has a silver lining.

It's always darkest before the storm.

After black clouds, clear weather.

When the night is darkest, the dawn is nearest.

All good things come to those who wait.

Faith can move mountains.

Modesty is the light of faith.

Forgive and forget.

Hope is the light of the world.

The best is yet to come.

Don't give up hope until hope is dead.

When one door shuts, another opens.

A mightier hope abolishes despair.

Hope is the nurse of misery.

Hope is the poor man's bread.

He who has hope has everything.

Don't feed yourself on false hopes.

Hope and a red flag are bait for men and mackerel.

Hope is the worst of evils, for it prolongs the torment of man.

Hope runs to infinity.

Mighty hopes make us men.

There's no hope for the wicked.

# ❧ Fate ❧

There's no flying from fate.

We make our fortunes and we call them fate.

Take things as they come.

Man proposes, God disposes.

If you don't like it, lump it.

Everyone is more or less master of his own fate.

You can't escape your fate.

Fate can be taken by the horns, like a goat, and pushed in
the right direction.

What's done is done.

No use crying over spilled milk.

What will be, will be.

You have to take the bitter with the sweet.

You can't win 'em all.

If you can't beat 'em, join 'em.

❧

# ⋄ God ⋄

God makes a nest for the blind bird.

God aids him who changes.

God fits the back to its burden.

God heals and the doctor takes the fee.

If God be with us, who shall stand against us?

The gods are on the side of the strongest.

The Lord helps those who help themselves.

Most men forget God all day and ask Him to remember
them at night.

God promises a safe landing but not a calm passage.

God puts food into clean hands.

God tempers the wind to the shorn lamb.

He who leaves God out of his reckoning
does not know how to count.

Nothing with God is accidental.

Pray to God, but keep hammering.

Where God builds a church, the devil builds a chapel.

Whom the gods would destroy they first make mad.

The mills of the gods grind exceedingly slow,
but they grind exceedingly fine.

Cleanliness is akin to godliness.

Better God than gold.

# ✣ Heaven and Hell ✣

Heaven takes care of children, sailors, and drunken men.

Hell and high water wait for no man.

The road to hell is paved with good intentions.

Hell and the courtroom are always open.

Better once in heaven than ten times at the gate.

Everybody that talks about heaven ain't going there.

Heaven helps those who help themselves.

Heaven protects the good man.

Some people are too mean for heaven but too good for hell.

Heaven keeps them who keep themselves.

Hell is never full.

Hell is full of sorry people.

Hell is full of good meanings, but heaven is full of good works.

Hell is truth seen too late.

# ⅏ Life ⅏

A good life keeps away wrinkles.

A long life may not be a good life, but a good life is long.

An ill life, an ill end.

Don't spend your life reaching for the moon.

For a long life, be moderate in all things, but don't miss anything.

If life were a thing that money could buy, the rich would live and the poor would die.

It's a great life if you can live through it.

Life and misery begin together.

Life begins at forty.

Life is just one damned thing after another.

Life is a mystery that death alone can solve.

Life is but a bowl of cherries.

Life is but a dream.

It may be your sole purpose in life is simply to serve as a warning to others.

Life is too short to waste on trifles.

Life is hard by the yard; by the inch, a cinch.

Life is made up of little things.

Life is no bed of roses.

Life is not a cup to be drained, but a measure to be filled.

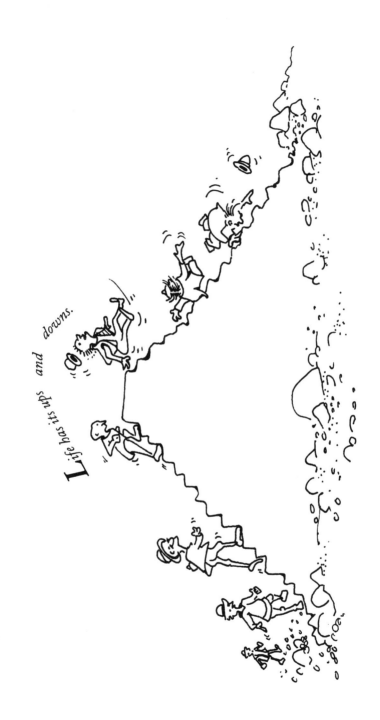

Life has its ups and downs.

Life is not wholly beer and skittles.

A short life and a merry one.

Life is what you make it.

Life's a gamble: you win or lose.

Simple things in life are best.

Live your own life, for you die your own death.

Plan your life as though you were going to live forever;
but live today as if you were going to die tomorrow.

The true value of life cannot be measured in dollars.

The secret of life is not to do what you like, but to like what you do.

You get out of life what you put into it.

Where there is life, there is hope.

The best things in life are free.

Into each life a little rain must fall.

Variety is the spice of life.

Live and learn.

Hope and fear, peace and strife, make up the troubled web of life.

Children and fools have merry lives.

# ᎀ Prayer ᎁ

Prayer is good for the soul.

Don't tempt providence.

Nightly prayer makes the day to shine.

Prayer keeps us from sinning; sinning keeps us from praying.

Some people who moan about prayers being answered don't seem to realize that the answer may be 'no.'

Courage is fear that has said its prayers.

Prayer should be the key of the day and the lock of the night.

Beware of the geese when the fox preaches.

The belly hates a long sermon.

ᎀ

*God helps the sailor, but he must row.*

69

# ❧ Pride ❧

Pride goes before fall.

Every ass loves to hear himself bray.

Pride and poverty go hand in hand.

Pride that dines on vanity supps on contempt.

Pride is a luxury a poor man cannot afford.

Pride often appears as humility.

The higher the hill, the lower the grass.

❧

# ❧ Truth ❧

This above all else: to your own self be true.

Truth will prevail.

Honesty is like an icicle: if once it melts, that's the end of it.

All fails where truth fails.

Ask me no questions and I'll tell you no lies.

A lie can go round the world while the truth is getting its britches on.

Lie down with dogs, get up with fleas.

Liars are not believed when they tell the truth.

Liars end by deceiving themselves.

A half truth is the blackest lie.

Out of the mouths of babes and drunks come the truth.

Always tell the truth, but don't always be telling the truth.

A lie well stuck to is as good as the truth.

Always tell your doctor and your lawyer the truth.

Honesty is the best policy.

Two wrongs don't make a right.

A lie stands on one leg, the truth two.

Truth is stranger than fiction.

Tell the truth all the time and you won't have to remember what you said.

Tell the truth if it kills you.

Don't measure your neighbor's honesty by your own.

Honesty pays.

Truth and oil always come to the top.

In politics a man must learn to rise above principle.

It is easier to fight for one's principles than to live up to them.

The greater the truth, the greater the libel.

The truth hurts.

Truth is mightier than the sword.

Truth may be blamed, but never shamed.

When in doubt, tell the truth.

Beauty is truth, truth beauty.

Truth shall conquer all.

African American culture supports a wealth of proverbs, with roots tracing back to slave quarters, Jamaica, and to other Caribbean societies. Still more of these proverbs have been derived from European culture, particularly from France and England.

In times of slavery, proverbs became a way for those enslaved to cope with inhuman conditions, to criticize captors, and to teach ways of survival. For African Americans today, proverbs continue to play an important role—communicating and preserving values, traditions, and wisdom for future generations.

# Uncle Remus's "Plantation Proverbs" (1881)

Better de gravy den no grease 'tall.

Rails split fo' bre'kfus'll season de dinner.

Lazy fokes' stummucks don't git tired.

De proudness un a man don't count w'en his head's cold.

Looks won't do ter split rails wid.

You can't tell much 'bout a chicken-pie till you git froo de crus'.

Don't rain eve'y time de pig squeal.

Ole man Know-All died las' year.

Meat fried fo' day won't las' twel night.

Ef you bleedzd ter eat dirt, eat clean dirt.

Dem w'at knows too much sleeps under de hopper.

Dem w'at eats kin say grace.

De pig dat runs off wid de year er corn gits little mo' den de cob.

Watch out w'en you'er gittin' all you want. Fattenin' hogs ain't in luck.

&

Norf wind know all de cracks in de house.

# African American Proverbs from the Quarters (1883)

Waitin' on de table is pow'ful way to git up appetite.

Folks on de rich bottoms stop braggin' when de ribber rise.

All de jestice in de wul' ain't fastened up in de cote 'ouse.

De fat beef ain't got much conferdince in de butcher.

You can't hurry up good times by waitin' for 'em.

A sunflower ain't so might putty in de dark.

૭

*Old goos sort o' s'picous 'bout
de feather-bed.*

# African American Proverbs from Texas

Evah bell yuh heah ain't uh dinnah bell.
*(A 'rising bell' called the slaves to work.)*

De one dat drop de crutch de bes' gits de mos' biscuits.
*(One who bows most politely has the easier job on the plantation.)*

You got eyes to see and wisdom not to see.
*(Slaves don't tell on each other.)*

Don' say no mo' wid you' mouf den you' back kin stan'.
*(Slaves should seldom speak.)*

Don't crow tel yuh git out o' de woods; dey mought be uh beah
behin' de las' tree.
*(A caution not to talk to anyone until you get to the
Underground Railroad.)*

# African American Proverbs
# from North Carolina

Barking saves biting.

A new broom sweeps clean, but an old brush knows the corners.

Set a cracked plate down softly.

A robin's song is not pretty to the worm.

One finger won't catch fleas.

The dinner bell is always in tune for a hungry man.

Get the candles lighted before you blow out the match.

# African American Proverbs Collected in Buffalo, New York (1980)

If you don't have the best of everything,
make the best of everything you have.

A hard head makes a soft ass.

If it don't fit, don't force it.

God gives you two ends; heads you win, tails you lose.

Do unto others, before they do unto you.

Keep your dress down and your draws up.

Don't forget where you came from.

If walls could talk, you'd know all.

You have to pay to play.

# Geechee Proverbs from the Sea Islands

Jes hold up your end er de beam a' de world'll roll on.

Day's short as ever, time's long as it has been.

Don't fly so high that you lit on a candle.

Trouble dollars sin as sho' as fever follers a chill.

One rain won't make a crop.

Live, learn, die and forget all.

A hard head makes a soft back.

# Creole Proverbs

Big blanket mek man sleep late.

What cost notin' gib good weight.

Dog hab shine tee' him b'long to butcher.

Greedy choke puppy.

Bull horn never too heaby fe' him head.
*(The back is fitted to the burden.)*

Too much sit down broke trousers.

Trubble neber blow shell.
*(Trouble happens without warning.)*

**Source:** Mieder, Wolfgang, ed. *American Proverbs: A Study of Text and Contexts.* New York: Peter Lang, 1990.

$F$ew Native American proverbs have been recorded among the rich cultures of America's aboriginal peoples, and there is little satisfactory explanation as to why this is so. Nonetheless, here is a sample of Indian tribal proverbs that have been discovered. For certain proverbs, explicatory notes are provided.

# Various Tribes

## Blackfeet

Never go to sleep when your meat is on the fire.

## Sioux

Would you choose a counselor,
watch him with his neighbor's children.

## Paiute

If a skunk walks in your trail and leaves a stink there,
do not go out of your path to prove that it is not yours.

# Southwest

*The moon is not shamed by the barking of the dogs.*

# Tsimshian

Go where your ears will be full of grubs.
*(A chiding for the self-destructive.)*

# Oklahoma Indians

The paleface's arm is no longer than his word.

There is no cure for the firewater's burn.

A squaw's tongue runs faster than the wind's legs.

Before the paleface came, there was no poison in the Indian's corn.

No Indian ever sold his daughter for a name.

The Indian scalps his enemy; the paleface skins his friends.

A starving man will eat with the wolf.

# Crow Indians

When pine needles turn yellow.
*(Characterizes an impossibility.)*

When cottontails have long tails.
*(Characterizes an impossibility.)*

He is like the turtle that was thrown into the water.
*(Said to he who pretends not to like what he really wants.)*

He is like the man who did not run away until after he had been scalped.
*(Refers to he who is belated in taking action.)*

*He is like the one who wanted to catch the porcupine.*
(Said to he who persists in a hopeless situation.)

# Chamula Tzotzil Indians

Hang your carrying bag over your shoulder well,
because I see that it is falling off.
*(Calls attention to an error in dress which could challenge the bearer's
masculine dignity.)*

It is going to rain; the cow is bawling.
*(May relate to atmospheric conditions, but also used to ridicule a woman
who cries in public.)*

The ram always throws himself around.
*(Said to ridicule the behavior of a drunk.)*

# Chukchi (Eskimos)

He repented of it even to his very buttocks.

Listening to a liar is like drinking warm water.
*(There is no satisfaction in it.)*

Even a small mouse has anger.

My temper is as smooth as sallow.

Not every sweet root gives birth to sweet grass.
*(Aleutian proverb.)*

**Source:** Mieder, Wolfgang, ed. *American Proverbs: A Study of Text and Contexts.* New York: Peter Lang, 1990.

Selected Proverbs By

# STATE

The following proverbs were first collected in the oral tradition of particular states. The states listed have been selected as being representative of certain regions of the United States. A few of the most popular proverbs may be repeated from previous categories to indicate their local origin.

# Arkansas

It doesn't take a big bone to choke a cow.

It takes gizzards and guts to get along in the world.

Even a blind hog will find an acorn once in a while.

A dead skunk still stinks.

Two wrongs never make a right, but maybe three will.

# California

When an attorney tries his own case, he has a fool for a client.

Don't wash your dirty clothes in public.

Crime does not pay.

Don't chew your cud twice.

An elephant never forgets.

What goes up must come down.

Don't rest on your oars.

A little knowledge is a dangerous thing.

There are tricks to all trades.

❧

# Colorado

Coffee boiled is coffee spoiled.

Bad news travels fast.

A shut mouth catches no flies.

It's the dry wheel that squeaks the loudest.

❧

# Hawaii

A lazy beauty is fit only for the dung hill.

The sand crab is small but digs a deep hole.

If you yawn while out fishing, you will get no fish.

One sees love after living together.

A good surf-rider will not get wet.

෨

# Illinois

Always is a long time.

You can't steal second base while your foot's on first.

Beware of he who has nothing to lose.

You can't judge a car by its paint job.

Once a drunkard, always a drunkard.

Diamonds come in small packages.

The only sure thing about luck is that it will change.

Don't get your plow in too deep.

Don't eat your pies before they're made.

෨

# Indiana

Business before pleasure.

Gospel is always better than law.

There is no rest for the wicked.

Every man has his price.

Nothing succeeds like success.

Half the world doesn't know how the other half lives.

# Kansas

The larger the body, the bigger the heart.

Gasoline and whiskey don't mix.

An old maid always knows how to raise children.

A wise man changes his mind; a fool never does.

The show must go on.

A wise woman never outsmarts her husband.

# Kentucky

Cigarettes are coffin nails.

Daisies won't tell.

When you dance you got to pay the fiddler.

One egg today is better than a hen tomorrow.

Speak in haste and repent in leisure.

The more you see some people, the better you like dogs.

The sweeter the rose, the sharper the thorns.

Better to wear out working for the Lord than to
rust out drinking for the devil.

There's no wool so white that a dyer can't make it black.

# Louisiana

Beauty is skin deep, ugly's to the bone;
beauty fades away, ugly holds its own.

It takes a carpenter to build a barn,
but any jackass can kick one down.

Another day, another dollar.

If you get into a fight with a skunk,
you're bound to come out smelling a little.

A whistling girl and a crowing hen always come to some bad end.

# Mississippi

Cows can't catch no rabbits.

A hen with biddies never burst her craw.

No telling which way luck, or a half-broke steer, is going to run.

A rolling stone gathers no moss, but it acquires polish.

A worm is about the only thing that does not fall down.

*The rooster can crow, but it's the hen that delivers the goods.*

# Nebraska

Beauty never boiled a pot.

Every bird likes to hear himself sing.

You cannot judge a book by its binding.

A dead dog tells no tales.

Don't kick a man when he's down.

Nothing makes money faster than money.

Success is two percent inspiration and
ninety-eight percent perspiration.

It takes two to make a match.

# New Mexico

Always sweep where your mother-in-law looks.

The best way to keep a nice-looking nose is
to keep it out of other people's business.

High-powered saddles ain't half as hard to find as high-powered
hombres to ride 'em.

If you don't C sharp, you'll B flat.

*If you've been near a skunk, don't say you haven't been.*

# New York

Reach for the high apples first; you can get the low ones anytime.

Economy is the poor man's bank.

Silks and satins put out the kitchen fire.

You can't expect anything from a pig but a grunt.

Don't send a boy on a man's errand.

# North Carolina

What ain't worth asking for, ain't worth having.

Make the best of what you have.

Home is where the heart is.

You never know the length of a snake until he's dead.

# Oregon

Don't stay until the last dog is hung.

Keep an ear to the ground.

The hand is quicker than the eye.

Hindsight is clearer than foresight.

Every man has an axe to grind.

It will all come out in the wash.

Water never runs uphill.

It's dog eat dog.

❧

*Curses, like chickens,
come home to roost.*

# Pennsylvania

Two apples a day keep heart ills away.

There's no shame in asking.

Babies must play.

You can't blame a fellow for asking.

Better to borrow than steal.

Always a bridesmaid, never a bride.

Save something for a rainy day.

Easy does it.

Jealousy will get you nowhere.

It's not what you know, but whom you know.

We learn something new every day.

Monkey see, monkey do.

You're only young once.

# South Carolina

It's a waste of lather to shave an ass.

A good beginning is half of the battle.

You can get the man out of the country,
but you can't get the country out of the man.

A poor excuse is better than none at all.

Findings is keepings.

An hour's sleep before midnight is worth two after.

Work while you work and play while you play.

# Tennessee

Sing before breakfast, cry before night.

A colt is good for nothing if it does not break its halter.

Two heads are better than one if one is a sheep's head.

Never tell a secret in the cornfield 'cause the corn's got ears.

# Texas

A bastard always looks like his father.

The cat is mighty dignified until the dog comes by.

He who watches the clock will be only a hand.

Corkscrews have sunk more people than cork jackets will ever save.

There's no such thing as the fastest gun.

The world owes you a living, providing you can earn it.

Don't kick until you're spurred.

# Vermont

Ancestors are a poor excuse for not amounting to a hill of beans.

Never cackle unless you lay.

Save your chips for kindling, not for wearing on your shoulder.

Every cider apple has a worm.

Good fences make good neighbors.

Anything worth having is worth fighting for.

A good word now is worth ten on a headstone.

The world is your cow, but you have to do the milking.

# Washington

The older the buck, the stiffer the horn.

No gains without pains.

Don't get caught up the creek without a paddle.

You can't win all the time.

Words are cheap.

It takes money to buy whiskey.

The train is never late except when you're in a hurry.

Don't run ahead of your shadow.

# Wisconsin

Childhood shows the man as morning shows the day.

All men are equal when they sleep.

They have rights who dare maintain them.

# *Other Proverbs from Hippocrene ...*

**Treasury of Love Proverbs from Many Lands**
*Illustrated by Rosemary Fox*
This anthology includes more than 600 proverbs on love from over 50 languages and cultures, addressing such timeless experiences as first love, unrequited love, jealousy, marriage, flirtation and attraction. Charming illustrations throughout.
**116 pages • 6 x 9 • illustrations • $17.50hc • 0-7818-0563-5 • W • (698)**

**Treasury of Love Quotations from Many Lands**
*Illustrated by Lizbeth Nauta*
This charming gift volume contains over 500 quotations from 400 great writers, thinkers and personalities—all on the subject of love. These are words of wit and wisdom from all over the world (over 40 countries and languages), from antiquity to the present day. With lovely illustrations throughout, this volume is the perfect gift of love for anyone.
**140 pages • 6 x 9 • illustrations • $17.50hc • 0-7818-0574-0 • W • (673)**

**International Dictionary of Proverbs**
*Gerd de Ley*
This comprehensive dictionary is a dynamic collection of 8,000 proverbs gathered from over 300 countries and regions. There is nothing in print today which resembles this reference dictionary's global scope and complete subject coverage. The proverbs are arranged alphabetically by country, and an index listing 2,000 key words is also provided. Gerd de Ley is an internationally-known author of reference books.
**hardcover: 437 pages • 5¹/₂ x 8¹/₂ • $29.50hc • 0-7818-0620-8 • NA • (706)**
**paperback: 437 pages • 5¹/₂ x 8¹/₂ • $19.95pb • 0-7818-0531-7 • NA • (656)**

## African Proverbs
*Gerd de Ley*
This extensive collection of 1,755 proverbs spans all regions of the African continent, revealing much about the wisdom, humor, and character of its people and culture. Each proverb is arranged alphabetically by key word and includes the country, province, or tribe of origin.
**124 pages • 6 x 9 • artwork • $17.50hc • 0-7818-0691-7 • W • (778)**

## Arabic Proverbs
*Joseph Hanki*
First published in Egypt in 1897, this collection contains 600 Arabic proverbs written in colloquial Arabic with side-by-side English translations; where appropriate, explanations are given of the custom which gave rise to the proverb. Many of these proverbs show a recognizable Biblical influence and are of great historical interest. Attractive, fascinating, and enjoyable, this book has many roles: reference guide, learning tool, and treasury of ethnic heritage.
**144 pages • 6 x 9 • $11.95pb • 0-7818-0631-3 • W • (711)**

## Irish Proverbs
*Illustrated by Fergus Lyons*
In the great oral tradition of Ireland, sharp-witted proverbs have been passed on for generations. This collection of over 200 proverbs recalls the experiences of Irish men and women in the cities, in the country, and by the sea. County Sligo native Fergus Lyons adds style and humor with 35 clever illustrations.
**104 pages • 6 x 9 • 35 b/w illustrations • $14.95hc • 0-7818-0676-3 • W • (761)**

## Scottish Proverbs
*Illustrated by Shona Grant*
Through opinions on love, drinking, work, money, law and politics, the sharp wit and critical eye of the Scottish spirit is strikingly conveyed in this collection. Glasgow artist Shona Grant illustrates the collection with 30 clever drawings.
**107 pages • 6 x 9 • 30 b/w illustrations • $14.95hc • 0-7818-0648-8 • W • (719)**

# *Hippocrene's Bilingual Proverbs Series...*

**Dictionary of 1,000 Chinese Proverbs, Bilingual**
*Schalk Leonard and Marjorie Lin*
125 pages • 5½ x 8½ • $11.95pb • 0-7818-0682-8 • W • (773)

**Dictionary of 1,000 Dutch Proverbs, Bilingual**
*Gerd de Ley*
131 pages • 5½ x 8½ • $11.95pb • 0-7818-0616-X • W • (707)

**Dictionary of 1,000 French Proverbs, Bilingual**
120 pages • 5½ x 8½ • $11.95pb • 0-7818-0400-0 • W • (146)

**Dictionary of 1,000 German Proverbs, Bilingual**
*Edited by Peter Mertvago*
123 pages • 5½ x 8½ • $11.95pb • 0-7818-0471-X • W • (540)

**Dictionary of 1,000 Italian Proverbs, Bilingual**
120 pages • 5½ x 8½ • $11.95pb • 0-7818-0458-2 • W • (370)

**Dictionary of 1,000 Jewish Proverbs, Bilingual**
*David C. Gross*
124 pages • 5½ x 8½ • $11.95pb • 0-7818-0529-5 • W • (628)

**Dictionary of 1,000 Polish Proverbs, Bilingual**
120 pages • 5½ x 8½ • $11.95pb • 0-7818-0482-5 • W • (568)

**Dictionary of 1,000 Russian Proverbs, Bilingual**
120 pages • 5½ x 8½ • $11.95pb • 0-7818-0564-3 • W • (694)

**Dictionary of 1,000 Spanish Proverbs, Bilingual**
120 pages • 5½ x 8½ • $11.95pb • 0-7818-0412-4 • W • (254)

All prices subject to change without prior notice. To purchase Hippocrene Books contact your local bookstore, call (718) 454-2366, or write to: HIPPOCRENE BOOKS, 171 Madison Avenue, New York, NY 10016. Please enclose check or money order, adding $5.00 shipping (UPS) for the first book and $.50 for each additional book.